FOOTPRINTS
I leave behind

Published by: TF Publishing

Paperback ISBN: 978-1-7384823-0-6
eBook ISBN: 978-1-7384823-1-3

Cover Design and Interior Layout by Spiffing Publishing.

FOOTPRINTS
I leave behind

TERENCE FLANAGAN

Chapter One
Glossop (1978–1981)

It all started in April 1978. I was born with cerebral palsy. That is when the oxygen does not go straight to the brain, resulting in brain damage. My balance is affected so much it may seem to anyone else that I am intoxicated; and I cannot walk for long as my legs become stiff and feel like concrete. My mother said I had epilepsy too, which I did not believe. I knew other kids with epilepsy that took medication. Without taking epilepsy medication people could die; it is not something you mess around with. Because my father was at the hospital when I was born, and the staff would have told him, how is that possible he did not know? Also, during my lifetime several doctors have looked at me strange when I said I had epilepsy. My mother had Munchausen syndrome by proxy, making out I was more disabled than I actually was. Munchausen syndrome is a mental illness and a form of child abuse.

The caretaker of a child, most often a mother, either makes up fake symptoms or causes real symptoms to make it look like the child is sick. I cannot say for sure, but she did have access to medication within a job she would get later on, and I believe she was drugging me to have seizures. Due to the mind games, my father did not know who the person my mother really was. I never had seizures at school or at my father's (my father did move out later) or outside the home. Epilepsy does not work like that and if you do not take medication, you are more likely to have more seizures. The doctor told my mother "Your son will never be able to walk" but as my mother was mentally unwell, I cannot say if this was the truth; maybe it was just another lie.

I had to wear a special helmet, which was my mother's idea. She had a lot of brilliant ideas (being sarcastic there). I hated it. I always removed the helmet as soon as I left the house. I did not need it in the first place. It was part of my mother's plan to get more sympathy.

We lived in a two-bedroom flat on Mersey Bank Road; me, my two sisters, mother, father. My father worked at Wall's meat factory as a security guard. I remember the Wall's sausages he would bring home. My mother was a stay-at-home mother. When I was four, she put me in a part-time nursery for an hour or two so she could work in a mental health unit. She was a secretary or helper; I am not really sure.

I remember my father would always come back home laughing and joking with us. He would make up bedtime stories about Superman or Batman, and I was always a part of the stories. My mother never did anything like that. It showed me that he loved me more than my mother. To make up stories to tell your kids at bedtime was a wonderful thing to do. My father was my hero. Then one day he walked out. It turned out my mother had been bullying my father for years. I think that changed him. My mother was a narcissist. She used people, including her own kids, as toys to discard whenever she got bored. He just had enough of being a doormat. He came back the next night, trying to get in to kiss his kids goodbye. He had to push my mother out of the way as she was making a scene on the doorstep. He ran up the stairs and kissed me, then left. I did not see him for a few months after that.

Chapter Two
New House (1981–1983)

We moved to a three-bedroom house down the road. My mother applied for a bigger council house because the flat was too small for me, and my sisters were sharing one bedroom. So, in the new house I got my own room which was good but that is when the abuse and neglect started as my father was not there to protect us and take the abuse himself.

My sisters were five and six years old and already my mother had them cooking, washing and ironing. I remember crawling into the kitchen. Because of my cerebral palsy it took me longer to learn to walk than most toddlers. I was four years old. My older sister was in there making my mother a cup of tea. She tripped over me, spilling the kettle and all the boiling water over my back. I was rushed to the hospital, and I nearly died. I do not know how, but I was not scarred. My sister got the blame, even though she was only six and had no place in the kitchen.

My mother used to make us watch horror movies like *Psycho*, *American Werewolf in London*, *Nightmare on Elm Street* and *V* the TV series and quite a few other movies; the list goes on. I bet if anyone asked her today, she would say it was their choice. What kid would choose to watch horror movies? Anyway, we could not go to bed till any movie was finished, or there would be trouble. Back then, parents still hit their kids; some were more comfortable with hitting than most. She found it funny, yet I was petrified for weeks. I did not want to sleep without the big light on.

We did have a dog in the house on Mersey Bank Road called Cleo. He was a golden retriever and we only had him a few days when police turned up at the door with his collar as a local farmer had shot him for being on his field. I blame my mother for this; for one, she did not like him, and two, she just left the door wide open. Again, someone felt sorry for us kids and donated the dog. I believe she took my dog to that farm knowing what would happen. I started feeling hatred towards my mother; I loved my dog.

She would leave us home alone for two to three days without food. My older sister would scrape mould off old food to feed us or go around the neighbouring house begging for food. My mother eventually got one of her friends to babysit us. The babysitter used to try and sneak food in for us, but my mother caught her. She never babysat for us again. I think the babysitter was depressed. I say this because she would play Diana Ross, 'I'm Still Waiting', over and over; so much so that when I hear it now it takes me back to when I was a kid. It is funny how music can do that. I believe the babysitter was a vulnerable person, and my mother saw this and took advantage of her, as this person would do anything my mother would say, maybe a bit of bullying too.

My mother started bringing guys back to the house. This would go on for years. Every Saturday, when my father picked us up to go to his house for the day, my mother and father would have a slanging match about all the guys she slept with before we would set off. She got a nickname around the village and not a nice one.

I was only really happy in school. How sad is that? I was embarrassed that all my clothes were old. I had no money for the tuck shop we had. My friends always tried to buy me things like crisps and pop, but I did not like to accept them. Still to this day I have never liked lending or borrowing, whether it's food or money.

Chapter Three
Narcissist (1983–1987)

We moved to a new house. It was on New Shaw Lane. The neglect got worse. The only meals we had were school meals and every Saturday at my father's house on Gamesley. My father did not know we were not being fed at home. If we had told him, he would have kicked off with our mother. The fighting between them got so bad that eventually my father stopped all contact with me and my sisters.

We were not allowed downstairs so could not watch television like other kids and were not allowed in the kitchen. They were out of bounds as downstairs belonged to her. My mother would take me to her friends' houses to show me off saying, "Look at my disabled son, don't you pity me?" I believe that's part of Munchausen syndrome by proxy. I felt like a dancing clown to perform whenever she wanted.

We all went to the Benefits Office in Manchester. Before we went, my mother would buy me new clothes – shirt, jeans, trainers, the works. On the way there she would tell me to fall a few times as the benefits people would be watching me walk, and I did as she said. You could not say no to my mother. When we got home, all the new clothes went back to the shop for a refund. Like I say, we never got to keep anything new; all the toys and clothes were hand-me-downs from our cousins. It is not like my mother did not have any money because she did – the benefits she was getting plus now she was getting disability benefit because of me. Both benefits went into two bank accounts: one was hers and one was mine. I know this because in the 1980s NatWest was giving out porcelain pig money jars if you opened an account with them. I had two pigs on my windowsill at home meaning she had two accounts; it was one bank account per person. But because she was my mother, she had access to my account. I never saw a penny. So, with all that money she still chose not to feed, clothe or buy toys for us.

I remember someone gave me a Rupert the Bear teddy and it was big, about four foot tall. My lovely mother cut a line down the back of it and pulled all the stuffing out. I was upset because I had never got anything like that before. She put me inside it after pulling all the stuffing out and sewed it up. My mother wanted me to get a picture with her friend's daughter – a nice picture of Rupert the Bear and the daughter, sitting on a bench – but it backfired as the little girl was petrified. It may have been out of good intentions for her friend but the way my mother went about it was a cruel thing to do, plus I had a challenging time breathing in that bear costume. When it was finished, she cut me out of it and put it in the bin, so did not bother to fix my bear for me. She could have put the stuffing back in and sewed it back up.

Chapter Four

Chocolates

I went to Fox Denton school, Oldham. It would take thirty minutes to get to school, there and back. I was in the second year, and was six years old, and I liked this girl called Louise. I had a little crush and wanted to get her a gift to show her how I felt, so I asked my mother to pick up some chocolates for me. She did the next day. I could not wait to give Louise the chocolates. Only it turned out they were liqueur chocolates. I felt like a right idiot. You may think that it may have been a mistake. No, my mother knew what she was doing, and when I got home, she was laughing.

Just to lighten things up, so it is not all doom and gloom, in the third year I was one of a few kids picked to give Princess Diana a bunch of flowers. When Princess Diana visited Oldham in 1987, two schools were invited – Fox Denton and Park Dean.

Fox Denton was a fantastic school; it was a safe haven where people cared about me and did not hurt or humiliate me like back home. I know a lot of kids did not like school, but I loved it. One day my mother paid a youth to steal my wheelchair so she could get sympathy. She contacted the local paper, and they came round to interview us. They did a piece on the local disabled boy who got his wheelchair stolen. I did not need a wheelchair in the first place. Like I say, I was not as disabled as she made out. My sisters knew the lad and got the information out of him about what my mother had done, paying him to take the wheelchair. My sisters can be a force to reckon with, especially when it comes to their disabled brother, but I was a child and I believed her. What child would not believe their mother?

We were at one of her friends where she would go every day for a cup of tea and toast. My mother did not want food in our house – or should I say her house – so was freeloading on this so-called friend as she could cut them off anytime at ease. Her friend had a painting on her wall above her fireplace. I do not know why, but I felt I had a connection to that painting. Maybe it was my past life, or I was too young to remember but I felt like I was that child. Like it really happened to me. It was a child in a shed looking at his mother, and as she was walking away abandoning him, he was crying. I know it was just a painting, but the feeling of abandonment would be with me through my childhood. My mother would use me to make people feel sorry for her. She enjoyed that feeling. She never paid for anything, food or drink, as people would buy her things out of sympathy. She would eat in front of us, knowing how hungry we were, and play stupid mind games with us.

Me and my sisters are not close because of our childhood. My mother used to make us fight each other for real, till there was blood; no play fighting. She dressed my sisters up and cut their hair, so they looked like boys, then sent them to school. I do not know what effect it had on them. All I will say is that my mother is evil. She left me in the middle of Ashton and Hyde markets and watched what I did. One time she left me in a café. I was six years old; she was hiding outside looking through the window. Why do that to a child? I can understand if it was an accident, but she did this about six or seven times. That was just cruel.

My father's family have a reputation, i.e, boxing runs in the family plus my father and uncles were bouncers. Because of that reputation, my mother would use it to bully people like she was a gangster, but quite often she would bully the wrong people and have to deal with the consequences. One day a guy came to our house with a hammer, wanting to smash my mother's face in because she was bullying his wife. She had sex with the guy so he would not beat the crap out of her. It would not occur to her to just stop bullying.

Christmases and birthdays were just normal days. Imagine looking out the windows seeing other kids playing with their new toys and new bikes and you got nothing, and no Christmas dinner or Christmas cake. I know my sisters felt the same as me. It was devastating; we were jealous of the other kids outside having fun.

It was around 1987 when my mother met the new guy. He had his own house and was a bit more upper class than the usual ones. My mother liked that lifestyle very much, as she was a council estate snob. The ones who had lived on council estates all their lives but think they are better than everybody else, like they are too good for that estate. One night, my mother and the boyfriend came back from the pub with fish and chips and just ate while dangling the food in front of our faces, as if to say, 'do you want some?'. I know that was my mother's idea. As he did not really know her cruel ways yet, I bet he thought it was just a joke. She would think that was funny.

They said kids do not get depressed, but I think that is rubbish. I would dream my real parents would come and get me from this cruel, nasty woman, because she took the wrong baby home from the hospital. How messed up is that?

Chapter Five

The Boyfriend (1987–1989)

We moved to her new boyfriend's house overnight. She met him, and we moved in. I would not say it was love at first sight – well maybe for him – but I know my mother does not love anyone. She wanted to get away from back home as her lies were catching up with her and people started to see I was not as disabled as she made out. And if that were the case, they would want their money back or whatever they gave my mother in charity.

The first night he gave us a Penguin biscuit, a packet of crisps and a can of Coke. It felt like Christmas. I know that sounds funny, but if you have never had chocolates, sweets or pop before you would understand.

On one hand he was kind, and on the other he could be cruel, like the fish and chips incident. Whether he thought that was a joke or not, he still joined in. So, moving there was a better quality of life, but the kindness he showed us could have been lulling us into a false sense of security. Getting me and my sisters to trust him before he took advantage.

The food had another meaning, it was like saying you are safe now; no need to go back to your old life. But there were dark intentions behind that.

Then, thirty minutes later they were fighting. My mother threw all his crockery at him. It turned out that she was cheating on him with my taxi driver who took me to school, so we moved back home. A few hours later my cousin woke me up, as the police were downstairs. I believe she took his money when we went back home, but this is only speculation. At this point, all I know for sure is that the boyfriend called the police, and we went back to his house. We would wake up to more fighting. Eventually, it all settled down and life seemed better. We had regular meals for once although my mother would start making pea and ham soup which was disgusting.

My school was happy, as they had warned my mother about not giving me breakfast a few times as I was falling asleep in class. I did not have the energy. Do not forget, I only had school meals before we moved to the boyfriend's house so did not eat anything at home.

They did tell her if it kept happening, they would call Social Services, and she always tried to blame my sisters making out she was too busy getting dressed. Before we moved to the boyfriend's house, one of my teachers did try to give me breakfast in the morning, but I said no as I was embarrassed, so I had an extra bottle of milk, as in the 1980s kids were given a bottle of milk before class in the mornings. I wish my school would have told Social Services sooner, as it would have saved us emotional stress.

My class went on a school trip to another junior school, and we took part in a few lessons. To my teacher's surprise, I kept up with the work. When we got back, they called my mother in to talk about this, as maybe I was in the wrong school. My mother did not like it because it did not suit her purpose of keeping me more disabled than I was.

Things at home (in the boyfriend's house) were better for a while. I finally could play outside like other kids, not in my bedroom all the time like before at home (in Glossop). But we did not see it coming; it was like we jumped out of the frying pan into the fire. Small things started to happen. The boyfriend's mood changed. It was like he was not interested in us anymore. Before, he would be joking around with us all the time. Then they started walking around naked. Seeing your mother naked is something no child should see. That was a bit weird. Then me and my sisters found some video cassette tapes. We wanted to watch a movie. It turned out they were porn videos of my mother and the boyfriend having sex. If people want to do that, it is up to them. But why leave them around when you have kids? Lock them away.

Things got worse as they started to have sex everywhere, inside and outside, not shy who saw them. I know we saw them a few times, and other people who were renting from the boyfriend saw them too. I can only assume they told them to leave. Some people have no shame.

We all went on holiday to Pontins, Prestatyn, Wales, and as soon as we got to the chalet my mother kicked us out, so you guessed it – having sex again. I was near the canal when some youth kicked me in. I could hardly swim. The canal was about two to three steps away from our chalet front door. I was shouting, but they did not come to my aid. I got out somehow, but they were still going at it. I had to wait outside soaking wet. I got the blame; my mother calling me a clumsy child. That was the last holiday I went on with them.

Later, the boyfriend would find me a place in a respite care home. I would start going there twice a fortnight for about six months. They had a remote-control robot there that was pretty fun and a BBC computer. I have always liked gaming and computers. What I did not know was that it was all planned to get me out of the way as he was a sexual predator. I cannot say too much about this as my sisters do not want to be in this. And I have to respect their decision. It got so bad we called Childline for help. The next day I came back home from school to see police and Social Services workers waiting for me. They quickly put me into a car and took me to the Social Services building to answer some questions. I did not really know anything at the time, only them having sex outside as they sent me to the care home out of the way. I will say I met a guy there who would later become my foster father. Anyway, after the questions I was taken to my grandma's to stay overnight. My sisters were there already. The next day we would be taken into care.

Chapter Six

Care (1989–1989)

Tall Turrets children's home was an old Victorian house that cracked and creaked and felt like it could fall down at any minute. The first night was scary. You are sharing a house with twelve strangers. Although I did make friends, nothing could prepare you for how lonely you feel even with other kids around you. Seeing kids in there with the same experiences as you felt good and bad; good that you were not alone and bad because it was heart-breaking. How could anyone treat kids like this? The feeling in the pit of your stomach, knowing no one loves you, is hard to understand. My family on both sides (father's family and mother's family) never came to visit. It was like we were outcasts for standing up for ourselves. They blamed us for going into care. It was like we tarnished the family name. How messed up was this? We were kids.

We moved there October/November time, so we were there for Christmas. Seeing other kids all going home is hard to see, and you are left behind. There were four of us out of twelve. The staff wanted us to start doing activities, and yes some were fun like swimming. There was one activity I told the staff member I could not do; it was a sixteen-mile hike around Dove Stone Reservoir. I told them I had cerebral palsy and could not walk that far. They just told me to shut up. John and Peter, who were two older lads, helped me out. Because of my cerebral palsy I can only walk so far then I cannot move. I think the staff thought I was lying so that means they did not read my file. (Every child in care has a file and that holds information on family life, health, medical needs.) So, the staff were not doing their jobs properly. All the other kids were just walking off and leaving me.

I would not say I hated it there, but I hated the staff. All of them had this attitude like they were too good to be working there and it was all our fault. There was a member of staff called John and he forced me to go on another hike in the woods. At this point I was sure he did not like me or any other disabled person as I was really struggling to walk. He tried to push me along to catch up with the others, but I fell back. He fell with me; his arm was on my shoulder, and he broke his arm. Now whose fault do you think that was? He came in the next day, arm in plaster, screaming at me. I told him he knew I was disabled and have problems walking yet he wanted me to go on these stupid walks.

After that, the best things about being there were making friends and the food. You would get meals, which were massive. I do not know why they cooked so much as half always went in the bin. And there was always a cake trolley that came around every mealtime. Food is my drug. Let me explain, when you have a childhood like mine, and your mother neglects you with food, it is hard to think of anything else except food. All we needed was a workhouse out of Oliver Twist and yes, my mother would have put me and my sisters in a workhouse if they were still around. Not feeding us was a type of control to keep us obedient. So, we went without certain foods for years and that is saying it lightly. When you do get introduced to a lot of food it can be overwhelming. It can also be a rush of excitement; just like drug users chasing that first hit, food can be the same – the first few minutes of eating makes you feel great then you come down and feel bad, and sometimes guilty. It is a fake feeling of happiness; it is more of a sugar addiction. I have been fighting this addiction for years, just like millions of others. I wonder if I had been given regular meals, even a few sweets as a kid, this addiction to food would not have happened.

A week later I was taken to Hyde Town Hall as my mother, her boyfriend and my sisters were all in court. I was too young to go – I was only eleven years old – so I just waited in the Town Hall with a social worker till it was over, meaning till they were out of court. My mother had to make a choice – have your kids back or stay with the boyfriend. She chose him because she did not want to go back to a council estate. It did not have anything to do with loving him, just that lifestyle. After everything, she turned her back on her own kids; it is not like we did not have suspicions that she did not love us, but this was like the final nail in the coffin. We did not see her for a few weeks after that.

Chapter Seven
Foster Placement (1989–1993)

I got some good news from my social worker. She asked if I wanted this move or to stay where I was in Tall Turrets. I jumped at the chance; I did not know at this point who the foster parents were, I just wanted out of that children's home. It turned out to be my old key worker from the respite care home my mother and her boyfriend sent me to get me out the way. I do not know how William and his wife Sarah found out about me ending up in care, but I was happy. It took about a week to move into their house.

The first night, William gave me some cassette tapes of *The Lord of The Rings* BBC dramatisation. I have been a fan ever since. I remember how quiet the first night was and every night after that. It is funny, in some ways I did miss the noise of the other kids. In the morning I came down for breakfast and we had chocolate croissants – they were delicious.

My mother would still come in and out of my life. She rang William one night saying, "Why did you steal my son?" I did not know this till years later; maybe William did not want to worry me or something, but how dare she! You cannot treat kids like dirt and expect to get them back, plus you chose your boyfriend over us, remember? A few days after that she said they were moving to Yarmouth, running away like the coward she is, never facing her problems.

Despite my family being a so-called hard family, they did not do anything about my mother's boyfriend. I am in two minds here; on one hand I can understand they did not want to get involved, and on the other we were their nieces and nephew. All I ever wanted was to be loved – is that too much to ask for? My father's family really never felt like my family, and I do not know why. It is like we were on the outside looking in. They were always together having parties. Whether it was birthdays or Christmas or on holiday, everyone was there having fun apart from me and my sisters. Again, what did we do wrong to any of you? Like I say, we were outcasts.

I went to Samuel Laycock School, and it was like everything happened all in the first year. I did not know about all that happened as I was left in the dark, people thinking I was too young to know the full truth. At the time, going into care, starting a new school, court case, mother running away. Back in the 1980s/1990s, parents used to threaten their kids that if you are a bad child we will put you in care. Other kids would ask me what I did to be put into care like it was a punishment. I never told them anything, but I guess if my old school friends end up reading this they will finally know.

It was coming up to my twelfth birthday. My father said he would come and take me out. I could not wait. He did turn up a few days later, just not on my birthday like he promised. I was looking out of the window all day. I loved my father more than my mother. Always did, from day one, so being let down by my father hurt me more than anything my mother could do. The next day William took me and some others to Camelot. It was a good day. I enjoyed the crazy golf, but it did not work; my father letting me down hurt bad. We had my birthday party at the weekend, and I had an old friend come over. I had never had a birthday party before, it was good.

Living with William and Sarah was like being in a normal family and the previous eleven years were just like a nightmare. William took me to London a few times, which I loved. We would go to Madame Tussauds and London Dungeon and the Transport Museum. Yes, I was happy for the first time, but I could not escape my past. I have a photographic memory, so I relive my past over and over again whether I want to or not. I sometimes think it would be great to forget, so after all this time, writing this can finally help me find a little peace.

Being in school was hard at first, as there were only three kids including myself in school that were in care; the other kids did not understand, and I did get bullied because of it. Some of my classmates came to my aid when they saw what was happening and there was no more bullying after that.

My foster parents' house was too small, so we started looking at bigger houses. We looked at a farmhouse in Oldham but because it reminded me of the boyfriend's house, I did not like it. We found one in Stalybridge ten minutes from my school. I got the attic bedroom; it was a great house. Things were good.

They took me to New York in 1990 and we stayed with their friend, Karan, in Connecticut. We went on a road trip from Connecticut to New York and from there to Philadelphia to Boston where we went humpback whale watching. After that we went to Washington DC before returning to Connecticut. We made two last stops, one to see the New York Yankees play baseball. I cannot remember the team they were playing. And the other on the way back from Boston, William and John (William's friend) surprised me by going to a drive-in. It's like an open cinema where you pull up to a big screen and sit in your car and watch a movie. The *Teenage Mutant Ninja Turtles* was playing; they knew I wanted to see it. John had to hold the car aerial to get the right signal to hear the movie.

It was a good time I will never forget. The day before we were going to fly back home, William took me to FAO Schwarz at Rockefeller Centre. That is where the floor piano was that Tom Hanks dances on in the movie *Big*.

Forward to 1993, we would go back to America but this time to Mississippi; one reason we were there was for Mardi Gras. The festival was good at the start, but it turned disappointing. It went from a family festival in Mississippi to New Orleans where it turned sleazy. We saw one guy dangling his private parts – not that I have anything against gay people, but this was a family festival with kids running about catching beads and candy (sweets). I did like America, and I made some good memories, but I was still a messed-up kid underneath.

Some of my school friends started getting jealous. It is like they forgot I was in a children's home before I was fostered. All they could see was the big house and holidays. I remember one teacher giving me a tough time, like with school activities. He did not want me to go on any because he thought I went on enough holidays with my parents (foster parents). He did not even check that one out; all my other teachers knew about me. He just thought they were rich, and I was just a spoilt brat. My foster father became a school governor but that somehow made matters worse. I honestly do not know what the teacher's problem was, and it was so far from the truth. Funny thing was, the teacher worked at another school where one of my sisters attended, so he knew my sister and did not put two and two together. Maybe if he did he would have known I was a care kid and not a spoilt brat with rich parents.

I was in my teenage years when I started acting out like most teenagers. I was moody and angry with everyone and that put a strain on my relationship with William and Sarah. I regretted that as I did not want to hurt them after all they did for me, but I have made amends with them now. But it should have never happened in the first place. I ran away to my father's the day after me and my foster parents argued about my behaviour and stayed there overnight as I did not know what else to do.

Chapter Eight
Mistake (1993–1994)

The next day my social worker came to my father's house and said I had a place in Hadfield House children's home, and he came to collect me. I do not know how but my mother turned up playing the caring parent, wanting me to run away and live with her. When my mother did come to see me in Hadfield House, she wanted to take me out for the day to spoil me. In her twisted mind, that was the way to win me over, thinking I would just say yes. How delusional is this woman? Back to reality, of course it was all about money. I don't know how people can get jealous over disability living allowance. We did go out, but I made her pick up my sisters because that is the person I am. I would feel bad seeing my mother behind their backs. She did not like that as there was no gain. She did not get anything out of seeing them, there was no love whatsoever.

She would turn up about five or six times over the next few years, asking the same thing like a broken record – to live with her – then disappearing just as fast as she arrived when I said, "No, I will never come to live with you. Why can't you leave me alone?" Everything is a game to her.

You will bump into other kids in care, three or four times in different homes. This one lad call Gordon, it seemed every place I moved he was there. He even shared the same social worker. He became a good friend. There are only a few good friends you will meet in your lifetime; all other so-called friends are quick to turn their backs on you at a drop of a hat. If you don't believe me, try lending them some money and see what happens. They will start by making excuses why they cannot pay you back. This is one reason why I find it hard to trust anyone. There were others you bump into, but I would not call them friends, more like acquaintances.

I was in Hadfield House just under six months, then moved to Kings Road children's home. I do not know why, but Social Services liked moving kids around like musical chairs. I did not stay anywhere longer than six months. It's hard at first living that way, but you get used to it, never really unpacking as it could be shorter than six months, maybe even three months so you're always ready to move. I went from Kings Road to a new foster placement in Denton, which did not work out. You sometimes get a foster placement where the carers only care about the money and not the kids in their care. I think it was about £450 a week per child, maybe less back then, so there was some who would take full advantage of that situation. It is sad but the truth that my carers in the new foster placement were like that. So, from there to Linden Road children's home, from there back to Kings Road children's home then to Tiverton House children's home. I was fifteen years old in Hadfield House and sixteen in Tiverton house so five moves was quite a lot in one year.

I was getting ready to leave care as you were only there till you were sixteen. I believe it's twenty-one now that you leave care which is a lot better than sixteen.

Chapter Nine
Aftercare (1994–1997)

The aftercare programme was being introduced around the same time I was leaving care, so I was one of the lucky ones. They got me a place in a supported shared house with another lad who had severe learning difficulties. He was a nice lad; both him and his sister lived at Kings Road children's home the same time as me, so I knew him before I moved in. I was there about two months then the aftercare worker got me a one-bed house in Hyde. It was great at first, but because I did not know how to cook properly or pay bills, I was a bit naive. They do not teach you life skills in care which I think is a mistake; not everyone has family or relatives to help out.

I made some mistakes letting some people stay over. The proprietor found out and did not like it as the house was a one-bed. It was my fault I got kicked out, I am not blaming anyone for this. But outside influences did not help the situation. Can you really trust anyone? I moved into a men's unit in Droylsden. I just stayed in my room. By that time I did not trust anyone, being let down by friends and family members over and over. I know it's partly my fault for letting them take advantage of me, and living there did not work out. Yet again people had a problem with my disability. Well I say that, they thought I was an alcoholic and there was a rule of no drinking on the premises plus I am not good with finances and that did get me into trouble. I ended up in two more hostels, both of which were full of drug users and alcoholics, not the safest places to live and yet the same things happen, always boiling down to my disability. I wish there were no discrimination against disabled people.

I was struggling with my mental health pretty bad. Living on my own just never really worked out for me. The people around me were into crime and drugs and I never wanted to be a part of that life. I did get involved in shoplifting for a while, but that is how I knew that life was not for me.

After some more mistakes (helping people who I thought liked me but who were really snakes), I ended up on the streets. Let me tell you, it was scary; people treat you like scum. You get a few who want to help, buy you food or drink and I do not mean alcohol, but others who will attack you for no other reason than they think they are better than you. If you are lucky, you can sleep all night without worrying about being attacked. I was only on the streets for three weeks in Ashton. That is not a lot, but plenty of time to know I never want to be in that situation again. When I was on the streets, me and a friend – I say that as you can make friends anywhere, even living homeless – broke into some vans a few nights just to get some sleep and get out of the rain. I know it was not the best thing to do, but when you're in that situation you do not care about the consequences. Apart from being attacked, another consequence would be you getting arrested, but then you would have food and a warm cell so it's better than the street. Not that I am saying I got arrested but it's not something you worry about. It is more like a backup plan; if something goes wrong at least you have a roof over your head. You have to learn how to survive. I was determined to find somewhere to sleep. I am not saying I am better than others but begging all day for pennies was not for me. After going to everywhere I could think of, I did get the door shut in my face once or twice – you know who you are.

I finally got a place in Rathbone Court in Rochdale. Rochdale was great, it felt like a new start. It was a care home for young adults, and I loved it. It felt like I was home. I understand why some prisoners want to go back to prison. It is not all about crime, but when you are institutionalised it is hard to shake off that feeling, even years later. I still long for it in all these places. (If someone becomes institutionalised, they gradually become less able to think and act independently, because of having lived for a long time under the rules of an institution.) That happened to me earlier on in the children's homes. When you live with many people there will be fights, as you make friends and enemies alike, some people just do not like you. My best friend was called Phillip; he was more like a brother then a friend, we did everything together. He had an accidental suicide. I was devastated and I still miss him.

I lived in Rathbone Court for three years before getting my own place. Because of my disability, I became a target for the local youths. This was in 1999. They wanted to use my flat as a drug den. This went on for a few months, and in all that time I got no help from the staff at Rathbone Court. The staff always thought I made up stories because how could someone so young have gone through so much and they did not believe I went to America. They did not help me to get out of that situation, neither did I get help from the police. Disability hate crime was still big back then and the police treated disabled people like second-class citizens. So, despite what the government says, disability hate crime has been around for years.

Chapter Ten
Back Home (2001–2023)

The only way to fix the problem was to become homeless, the one thing I never wanted to happen again. I got a place in a mental health hostel with the help of an old social worker. He took pity on me and helped me get into the hostel back in Tameside. The managers of the hostel were ripping residents off; most of them had mental health problems or learning difficulties. I got some backdated disability benefit; they tried selling me a TV unit and a couch, but anyone could tell they were really old and marked. Taking advantage of people in your care is simply wrong. I needed to move out but before I left, I did tell them what I thought. I applied for a council flat, but it is like my problems follow me wherever I go.

Because of my disability, some see me as an easy target. The guy underneath my flat started causing me trouble.

He thought he was hard because he hung around with a group of youths; I guess kids will do anything for sweets. He got them to smash my front door in with a hammer, while he banged on his ceiling. This happened day and night. Because of my backdated money I had enough money to go private renting. Me and a friend shared the rent. The house was in poor condition. Turned out our property owner was a rogue proprietor. Because of the situation, I started getting more panic attacks then normal. I have always had panic attacks since I was a kid, but now they were ten times worse. I could not keep up with the rent. I was trying my best not to have a mental breakdown as problems were starting to get on top of me.

I got another housing association two-bed flat (this was before the bedroom tax). I wanted to have a better life like other people, so I tried getting help to get into work. Remploy helps disabled people to find work so I met one of the workers there and he said he could help me out. I told him, "Please do not put me in a situation without walking me through it first as I would just panic." He said no problem. The next day he rang me up saying I had a mock interview with Royal Mail. I did not like it, as he did what I asked him not to do. So, I needed to go and buy all new clothes as I did not have shirt, tie, trousers and shoes. Then the next day I made my way to their central office in Manchester. It turned out they invited too many people for this mock interview. I was not happy plus all the others were wearing t-shirts and jeans. After all that effort, they told me just to go home but thank you from coming. What a joke. It was now raining hard. Walking back into Manchester to get the bus home I had the biggest panic attack of my life – hard to breathe, dizziness, chest pains, feeling you are going to die in that bus stop. Everyone running to get shelter out of the rain, and people staring at me just trying to get on the bus and get home. It was a nightmare. I have never been to Manchester on my own since. If you have a panic attack in a certain place it can stop you going back there out of fear of having another one. When your anxiety is like this, a million thoughts go through your head like you could die, or someone could do you harm – the list goes on. My worst day, I would have three to four panic attacks. Having one a day is bad but four is horrendous. I would wake up most mornings hating the world and everyone in it, including myself. People talk about forgiveness and God. I want to believe, I really do, but all I see are snakes and backstabbers. I do not like feeling like this, but I do not know how to fix this problem. Maybe I am doomed to live like this till the end.

Parents that treat their kids like crap should die. My mother went through the care system so you would think she would try harder not to repeat what her parents did to her. I needed help and there was only one person I trusted, so I called him. William. He came around, and I was a mess. I broke down crying. Despite what I did all of those years ago to him and his wife, I am grateful to them both. William was helping me with shopping. One day in Tesco I had a panic attack. I suddenly grabbed his arm. Poor guy, I must have scared him. I am physically sick after every panic attack. If I do not empty my stomach that will lead to another panic attack, I do not know why. I apologised to William. I was embarrassed he saw me like that, and yes, I know it is not my fault. I would not wish panic attacks on anyone.

Chapter Eleven

The Reunion with My Father (2019–2021)

My father came back into my life recently. I know me and my father did not agree completely on some things, but I did love my father. It is strange seeing this strong guy who is now old and vulnerable and a little bit scared of the outside world. To tell you the truth, I did not like seeing him like that. I was happy I got the last few years getting to know him again. He did say he was proud of the person I have become. I have been waiting my whole life for him to say that. I am thankful we were able to come to an understanding before he passed away. Feeling your parents do not love you is hard to explain. It is like you feel empty inside and believe me it does not leave you. If you let it, it can take you to a dark place, especially when you see other people with their families having good times with each other and you are all alone.

I am forty-five now and still feel like a kid when I see people together. I sometimes feel lost, like there is no hope. I find it hard trusting people and I do now suffer with agoraphobia. I am trying my best to overcome this, but it is like fighting a brick wall. I am talking about my problems now instead of bottling them up.

Chapter Twelve

Life Lessons

1. PTSD does not only affect army personnel. It affects anyone who suffers trauma, including kids in care. I had friends who committed suicide because they could not cope with their pasts and never got the right help. I have talked to a few therapists in my time, and most do not understand, and some can be very patronising. I will say the ones that understand are the people who have been through similar experiences. There should be more help for kids and adults who have been through the care system, like life skills when I came out of care. I did not know anything. Yes, there was an aftercare team, but they really did not help, just dumped me in that house in Hyde and left me to it. I got income support every two weeks but because I did not know about budgeting, I spent it on rubbish. I think they should teach

you the life skills you need before you leave care. It is great that you get help till you're at least twenty-one now, as when I left it was sixteen and that was too young. Like I said before, not everyone has people around them to help so learning life skills is important.

2. I am alone because I do not want to get hurt again and that is no way to live. Some people think that is weird. I am just protecting myself even though it is all in my head and I know there is no real danger outside. I think I sometimes can be emotionally detached because of my past and some people take that as I do not care. But that in itself is emotional damage. I wanted to write my story because I do not want to talk about my past anymore. Every new person you meet wants to know about your past and you get a bit sick of talking about it over and over again. I know I did and in part to let people know you are not alone and not everyone gets that happy family lifestyle. I see so many people come from the care background without a voice. I am not saying I have a voice but without someone saying this nothing will improve. A lot of ex-care kids fall through the cracks and are forgotten about in society. I am a gamer, and when I get stressed, I play video games – that is how I cope. Other people read books, play music or watch movies, whatever works

for you. Some years ago, I joined a mental health charity called Making a Difference Tameside. They have a café and a skill centre. It can serve different purposes, whether it is learning life skills or just talking to someone. The woman who runs it is called Janice. I started baking cakes and I quite enjoy it. From cheesecake to carrot cake, I find baking helps me to forget my troubles for a few hours. I find it tranquil.

Final Chapter

Forgiveness

If I have hurt people writing this, I do apologise. That was not my intention. This book is not about blaming anyone. I have been carrying the weight of my past on my shoulders for far too long now. As Eminem says, cleaning out my closet. I may not look it, but I feel old. A difficult life takes its toll and all I want is to be free and live a happy life if that is possible. You can be a victim of your past or you can turn it around and say I am a survivor. I am a lot stronger than I realise.

Although life has been extremely difficult and caused a lot of physical and emotional pain, it has been a journey in which I have learned many good things, met new people who had my best interests at heart and wanted to see me succeed. I am now in a more positive place in my life, looking to the future with hope and purpose.

Through the people who care about me, I am finding who I really am, my identity, my character and personality, that I can do good things, I am creative. I can see now I am an okay person. Loved and cared about, an important person. As for my mother, she still does not think she did anything wrong. It took me a long time but now I see through her narcissistic ways. I do not hate her, but it does not mean I like her either. I have forgiven my mother, but she is a deeply unhappy woman. I really hope she can get the help she needs but I do not think that will happen. I hope in time she can forgive herself.

I would like to thank William and Janice who helped me with this book.

THANK YOU FOR TAKING TIME OUT TO
READ MY STORY, I DO APPRECIATE IT, AND I
HOPE YOU CAN LEARN FROM IT

Printed in Great Britain
by Amazon

46051075R00030